BRIAN WHITTINGHAM, born and living in Glasgow, is a poet, playwright, fiction writer, editor and creative writing tutor. Recent poetry collections include *Drink the Green Fairy* and *The Old Man From Brooklyn and the Charing Cross Carpet*. Recent plays include *Smugglers and Black-Damp* and *The Devil's Dandruff*. In 1994 Brian was awarded a month's fellowship in Yaddo artists' colony in Saratoga Springs, New York where he co-wrote *Diamonds in Bedlam* with Glasgow songwriter, Willie Black, which they performed during the *Birth of Impressionism* Exhibition in Glasgow. In 2000 he won first prize in the *Sunday Herald* Short Story Competition. His poems and stories have been widely published in anthologies and magazines. A former steelworker/ draughtsman, he performed his steel-working poems as part of the BBC's 'Ballad of the Big Ships Live' in Glasgow's Royal Concert Hall in 2007. He has performed and lectured in the UK, Europe and the USA, in places as diverse as beaches, universities, prisons, pubs, schools and colleges. He is currently a lecturer in creative writing at Glasgow's College of Nautical Studies.

MANDY SINCLAIR was born in Coatbridge, Lanarkshire. She studied at Glasgow College of Building and Printing, where she was awarded the prize for illustration. She now works as a freelance illustration tutor for Renfrewshire Council's Out of School Learning Group, whose anthology, *The Ocean Calls the Tide* was published in 2006. She also works for Glasgow City Libraries, and her present project is a children's picture book called *Princess Shriekarina*. She lives in Erskine with her husband and two children and is a member of The Erskine Writer's Group. She enjoys walking the dog while pondering on the possibilities of constructing a time machine.

Brian Whittingham has a brilliant track record of working with schools. His work for Glasgow Museums brought exhibitions alive and drew pupils into the collections in new and exciting ways. The poetry helped children express their thoughts and emotions in ways that those of us who have watched Brian at work couldn't begin to imagine. This collection will inspire, delight and inform all who dip into it.

ANNE WALLACE, *Education Officer, Glasgow Museums*

Brian's ability to capture experiences through sensory imagery is enhanced by the beautiful illustrations. These would keep even the most reluctant of young readers mesmerised.This is a rich and entertaining poetry collection that can be used as a resource that teachers would welcome in the classroom.

MAURA MCROBBIE, *Primary Teacher and Enterprise Support Officer, West Dunbartonshire Council*

A wonderful anthology of poems which assaults the senses and captures the heart. The subject matter, the humour and the evocation of time and place would appeal to even the most apathetic reader; yet there is more than enough to simulate the more capable. I would highly recommend this collection to my colleagues as a classroom resource.

CLAIRE CHISHOLM, *Principal Teacher of English, St Andrew's High School, Clydebank*

Septimus Pitt and the Grumbleoids

Poems by
BRIAN WHITTINGHAM

Illustrations by
MANDY SINCLAIR

Luath Press Limited

EDINBURGH

www.luath.co.uk

First published 2007

ISBN (10): 1-905222-81-5
ISBN (13): 978-1-9-05222-81-0

The paper used in this book is recyclable. It is made from
low chlorine pulps produced in a low energy, low emission manner
from renewable forests.

Printed and bound by
Scotprint, Haddington

Typeset in 10 point Sabon

Contents

Introduction

When the child inside you wonders: how you can send letters to a pen-friend in Saturn; what sort of things you could do with a rainbow; what might your fate be if you ate all the sweeties in an ice cream van; who is the mysterious stranger who walks around Glasgow carrying a football with him wherever he goes; if you were a ghost without a name, what problems might you come across in life; what would happen to you if you were to complain about things all the time; how teachers can actually dress the way they do; what the darkness might say to you if it could speak; who the mysterious being is who wanders around Glasgow's Mitchell Library in the evenings when everyone has gone home; and, still in the Mitchell Library, what happens when a puppet-master stores his ancient puppets there; who was the employee of Glasgow's People's Palace that had fur, ate cockroaches and crawled about on all fours; what noises annoy grown-ups; and what industry Glasgow had that involved Three Queens. Read on and find the answers to these questions, and many more, in this book of poetry that will be the envy of your friends and will bamboozle your parents.

Brian Whittingham

Catch a Rainbow

If I could catch a rainbow

I'd hang it round your shoulders.
A rainbow scarf.
Its pot of gold
next to the beat of your heart.

If I could catch a rainbow

I'd make
rainbow puddles.
For you to splash colour
wherever your steps may take you.

If I could catch a rainbow

I'd turn it upside down.
A rainbow rocking bed
to let you float to a land of bliss,
drift safe on dozing dreams.

If I could catch a rainbow.

Fizz-Whizz Space Dust

Have you ever been rippled
by the ice cream man
who jingles down the street
in his multicoloured van?

Playing crazy tunes
as he drives round the schemes
with his rainbow ripple-juicer
filling you with tasty dreams.

He'll fill you with...

	Irn-Bru chews.
and	Screwball cones.
	Rainbow nerds
and	Caramac
	candy floss
and	Fudgerydoos.

Annnnd...   Parma Violets,
               Sherbet Fountains,
               Flying Saucers,
               Rainbow Crystals,
               Monster Munches,

Or maybe... Bazooka Joe bubblegum
Or............ Bubblicious bubblegum
Or............ Sour-Apple-Green-Howler bubblegum,

Or maybe even... fizzy vampire teeth

But – beware of...

Fizz-Whizz Space Dust

if you don't want an exploding tummy, that is.

The Keepie-Uppie King

The Keepie-Uppie King
The Keepie-Uppie King
The Keepie-Uppie
    Keepie-Uppie
    Keepie-Uppie King.

    His robe's a Scotland football top
    his name emblazoned on the back,
    his treasure is the football
    he carries inside his pack.

The Keepie-Uppie King
The Keepie-Uppie King
The Keepie-Uppie
    Keepie-Uppie
    Keepie-Uppie King.

    His kingdom is Glasgow's George Square
    his crown, headphones on his head,
    his ball could be a jester's
    with its silver stripes and red.

The Keepie-Uppie King
The Keepie-Uppie King
The Keepie-Uppie
    Keepie-Uppie
    Keepie-Uppie King.

    He holds his subjects in his spell
    flicking the ball from foot to thigh
    to chest to shoulder to neck to head,

    holding court is easy-peasy,
        he doesn't even have to try,
        he doesn't even have to try.

The Keepie-Uppie King
The Keepie-Uppie King
The Keepie-Uppie
    Keepie-Uppie
    Keepie-Uppie King.

The Cosmic Postman

Are you the cosmic postman?
Are you of the human race?
Your territory the cosmos
where you whoosh through outer space?

Maybe you come from Venus
with acid in its clouds,
where volcanoes explode
with eruptions ever so loud?

Or maybe you come from Mars
covered in thick red dust?
Is it so, if you move too slow,
you seize up, then rust?

Or do you come from Saturn?
And do you feel like a king
with your postman's bicycle
cycling round its rocky rings?

Then again maybe Neptune
The planet full of storms
Where it's so blue and icy cold
you can never, ever be warm.

Wherever you come from
make sure the post's never late
even when there's a ...

Beware of Alien Dog

sign on every garden gate.

Are you the cosmic postman?
Are you of the human race?
Your territory the cosmos
where you zoom through outer space?

The Grumbleoid Rap

They're the grumbling Grumbleoids
they live in Grumbletown,
their aim in life has always been
to put everybody down.

'cause that's where they're at – yo!
that's where they're at.

Whether you're tall, whether you're small
whether you're fat or thin
they want you to feel horrible
so you can never win.

'cause that's where they're at – yo!
that's where they're at.

They complain about everything
the sun, the rain, the snow,
they even complain about complaining
wherever they may go.

'cause that's where they're at – yo!
that's where they're at.

Why are they always nasty?
Why are they always bad?
Because being a grumbling Grumbleoid's
the only pleasure they've ever had.

'cause that's where they're at – yo!
that's where they're at.

'cause that's where they're at – yo!
that's where they're at.

see notes

Dress Sense

You shoulda seen the new teacher
by the way,
pure crazy looking so he wiz.

He hud a mad ponytail
tied wi a kinda elastic band
so he did.

An these pure crazy
purple-tintit glasses,
and this tartan waistcoat,
pure bright silky like,
the whole class wiz blinded by it
so they wur.

It was pure whoaaaaaaaaawee!

Then this green jaiket
with rid bits aw ower it
the kind you widnae be seen dead in
by the way.

Then his Doc Marten boots
with the wee totey labels
looked stupit so they did.

An he pure takes oot
wan ae they luminous watches
by the way.

Then *he* tells *us*
tae pay attention
and I hud to look the other way
at Julie
who was pure guttin hersel
by the way
...pure guttin hersel.

Mister Nobody

I'm a spook from the toilets
I'm the ghost without a name
a head without a body
it's really a crying shame.

I'm not on the ghoul register
I never get near a class,
the janitor just ignores me
won't even give me a visitor's pass –

No name you see!

I still do what a spirit does
I scream and screech and wail
blow my frosty misty breath
and scare spooked pupils pale –

With fright you see!

Keen to state my spectre's case
I've a meeting with the head
but I don't hold out too much hope
he'll remind me I'm already dead!

Perhaps *you* could help me out
any name you think of would do
then I'd be allowed to come to class

and sit

right here

right next

to you!

I Am The Dark

Late at night if you
open the bedroom door
I leak into the hall.

If you go downstairs
I'll be there, waiting.

If you peek from behind the curtains –

You'll find me
        out of reach of searching street lights
You'll find me
        in the sky speckled with starry dreams
You'll find me
        inside the sleepy corners of your head.

I have many friends –

The reflections in puddles
that wobble like multicoloured jellies
when you stamp splash them.

The fireworks that explode
rainbow bursts
and drizzle dripping silver.

The night-time animals
that slumber daytime dreams
waiting for the sun to be tucked in by the moon

and the wished upon stars
that glimmer at their brightest
when I am at my blackest.

Septimus Pitt

I am an eternal guardian.

Three floors deep below the ground
I feed on discarded
words of yesterdays.

My steps leave no footprints,
are silent as years gone by.

When not napping in my chair,
Inky, my faithful companion,
follows me through dark corridors of gloom

her pointed claws
sharp as a vampire's fingernails.

She scrapes and scratches after
night-time things
that creep and crawl,
night-time things
that might munch their way
through a feast of dry tasty pages,
given half a chance.

Sometimes,
when the staff have left
for their cosy librarians' homes
slipping on their cosy librarians' slippers,
sipping on their cosy librarians' cocoa,

I climb to the upstairs floor,
walk on its black and white linoleum squares.

Like a lone chess piece
I wander, exploring,
unable to touch crisp pages
of new books, I sniff their scent,
Inky purring silently by my side

in the still library
filled with the air of yesterdays.

see notes

In Between Sherbet Dabs

In between sherbet dabs
and kick-the-can.

amongst manky middens

short-trousered urchins
hoist imaginary treasure chests
on board pirate ships.

They send coded messages
through tin-can phones
from their secret den.

They spook unexpected visitors
with howling wails
in haunted houses.

A tightrope walker balances on a dyke
decorated with chalk graffiti proclaiming

Johny Currie loves Mary Bennet.

In between Acid drops
and hunch-cuddie-hunch

Back-court madams with pink-
flowered aprons, grown-ups' high heels
and oversize coats
pushing and shooshing dolls in prams.

Their make-believe shops with
upturned wooden-box counters
tins, bottles and weeds – potions, lotions and flowers
and old saucers with clabber-butter.

Paid for with broken-plate pieces
some with gold-rimmed edges
and the make-believe mammies
making sure there was no short change.

In between aniseed-balls
and peever-beds

as assorted chimneys
prod and poke the grey sky
leaking snakes of smoggy smoke.

* see notes

The Retired Puppeteer

The retired puppeteer
who looks a bit like Mister Punch
tells us,
his audience,

'At night, the ancient puppeteers
stored the puppets' heads
separate from their bodies…
made from wood you see,
a living thing.'

He tells us,

'In the beginning
before the puppets,
even before writing,
storytellers in Egypt, Greece, India and China
told their tales
with movement of the hands.'

He demonstrates.

He slowly spreads extended fingers
to represent a rising sun.
His hands scribe a circle in the air
to represent the Earth.
He waggles dragging fingers
to represent a free-flowing river.

He prompts us
to follow suit with his next example,
and, as if manipulated by strings from above,
we all place palm on palm
under our inclined heads
and mimic sleeping a slumbering sleep.

All the while,
his retired slack-stringed marionettes
slouch in the lecture theatre's corner
watching us with hooded eyes
like half-drunk actors
frozen offstage
awaiting their cue to come to life.

Sister Smudge

In the People's Palace,
Sister Smudge, a rodent operative
with a black smudge beauty spot
under wise wily whiskers

wanders the Winter Garden
where woolly-coated fern trees
lean and eavesdrop on her thoughts
amongst plant blossoms that splash
colour dripping as if from a painter's palette.

> Sometimes Sister Smudge will be pristine,
> other times, pure manky,
> as she wanders into the Palace inspecting

> or curling up for a nap
> on the tobacco lord's tabletop
> ignoring his stuffed importance.

> And sometimes
> she sharpens her claws
> on the 18th-century hessian wall

making ready for her foray
into the house of glass
and her evening meal
of mice and giant cockroaches
that scuttle around

the cacti's spiked leaves
that lick the air
with their hungry jagged tongues.

* see notes*

Daein Ma Box In

Gonny stoap makin that noise?
It's daein ma box in.

Whit noise is that Maw?

That, click click click click clickin
That thing yi dae wi the tap o yir pen.

That, bang bang bang bang bangin
That thing yi dae wi the side o yir shoe.

That, thump thump thump thump thumpin
That thing yi dae wi yir baw against the wa.

That, chomp chomp chomp chomp chompin
That thing yi dae when yi eat yir grub.

That tap tap tap tap tappin
That thing yi dae wi yir fingers
oan the tap o the table
when aw ah'm tryin tae dae
is get some peace an quiet.

Ah don't ask fur much,
Aw ah'm askin is, ur yi gonny – stoap – makin – that noise?
It's daein ma box right in.

But Maw... it's no daein ma box in neither it is.

No daein ma box in!

The Clay Tiger

I'm a clay tiger, woman-made.
I'm muscle and blood.

I'm an earth-brown red
as if the colour of my heart
has become the whole of me.

I'm surrounded by watercolour brothers
hiding in their artists' jungles.

I have no bones man can use
      to grind into tonic
        that he thinks cures his headache.
I have no whiskers man can use
      to boil into lotion
        that he thinks cures his toothache.
I have no flesh man can use
      to bubble into medicine
        that he thinks cures his bellyache.

So, for the moment I'm safe,
still, always on my guard.

See how I'm ready
crouching
poised, prepared to pounce, if required,
on the most dangerous of animals.

* see notes

The Three Queens

In the display case
sit three queens.

Large scale models
that will never see
large scale oceans.

They have…

> no buzz of passengers' cheering cheerios,
> no blasting horns piercing sea-salt air,
> no fluttering flags waving at winds,
> no propellers churning gloomy depths,
>> or screeching gulls
>> wheeling for tit-bits
>> discarded by the well-heeled.

Instead
their deserted decks
tower above
placards with chalked legend…

Queen Mary (Hull 534)
A ghost ship eventually completed
by depression-hit, cloth-capped artisans.
A 30s symbol of hope for the hopeless?

Queen Elizabeth (Hull 552)
A sister to meet the demand of the 40s
of weekly Atlantic crossings
by the likes of Churchill, Chaplin and Crosby.

Queen Elizabeth 2 (Hull 736)
The final Clyde-built liner
destined for a Caribbean old-age
due to the new fangled jet-planes of the 60s.

And all are surrounded
by appropriate memorabilia…

Faded launch cards at 15 shillings a seat.
Cunard books of matches.
Engraved crystal goblets.
A propelling-pencil purchased on ship.

And, once held
by Queens Mary and Elizabeth,

a set of silver-handled scissors
decorated with silver seahorses

     no longer cutting silky ribbons,
     releasing bottles of bubbly
     to smash against hulls,
     their champagne froth
     dripping on to the greased slipways below.

see notes

Michael and Billy

lived next door tae each other;
wur ages wi each other

and oan Seturdays
baith goat lifted ower the turnstiles.

Michael at Parkheed
wi his faither wavin a tricolour,
singin '...the bayonets
slash, the orange sash...'

Michael smilin when he wis callin Billy a hun,
tellin him, he'd never walk alone.

Billy? He'd go to Ibrox
wi his faither wavin a Union Jack,
singin '...the old orange flute
played the Protestant boys, tooraloo, tooraloo...'

Billy smiled, callin Michael a pape,
tellin him, he wis a son o' William.

Oan Sundays, they played fitba
oan the cinder park.
Bunched-up jumpers as goalposts.
Ten twenty-waners.

Michael? He wis always Billy McNeill – *Cesar*.
Billy? He wis Boabbie Shearer – *Captain Cutlass*.
An in goal wis always skinny-malinky Pat,
he wis Lev Yashin, *the Black Spider*.

Cesar, *Captain Cutlass* and *the Black Spider*
gaun up the road thegether at the end o' the day.

* see notes

Notes

THE GRUMBLEOIDS

Do you know of any Grumbleoids? You could do a drawing of
Grumbletown. We should feel sorry for Grumbleoids, who, because of
their constant complaining, miss out on the real happiness of life, but we
should also beware that we don't turn into a Grumbleoid ourselves, or we
would have to move house and end up living in Grumbletown.

SEPTIMUS PITT

Septimus Pitt was one of the first librarians in Glasgow's Mitchell Library.
He died, in the Library, in 1937, as did Inky the Library cat. The ghosts of
Septimus and Inky were destined to haunt the basement corridors for
eternity, and can, on occasion, still be seen to this very day.

IN BETWEEN SHERBET DABS

From paintings (in Provand's Lordship, the oldest house in Glasgow),
by Thomas McGoran, a retired railwayman, who was inspired by his
childhood memories of growing up in a tenement in the East End of
Glasgow in the 1930s.

SISTER SMUDGE

Smudge, the People's Palace cat of 1979 to 2000, was initially employed as
a rodent operative and became a member of the General, Municipal and
Boilermakers' Trade Union, after being refused admission by NALGO as a
blue collar worker. Her territory was the People's Palace and the Winter
Gardens where she carried out her inspections and kept the rodent
population under control, though she did nothing about the pigeons
whom she deemed to be below her station and not worthy of her
attention. She became a celebrity, having her own range of memorabilia
that can now be found scattered throughout the continents of the world,
courtesy of cat-loving Glaswegians.

THE CLAY TIGER

Inspired by a plaster sculpture titled 'Muscle and Blood' by Nicola Hicks,
exhibited in the 'Wild Tigers of Bandhavgarh' exhibition at the Burrell
Collection in 2000.

THE THREE QUEENS

This poem is taken from models of the Three Queens that are housed in Glasgow's Museum of Transport. The author, Brian Whittingham, left school at 15 in 1965 to start work in John Brown's shipyard in Clydebank. Shortly after, along with thousands of others, he began working on Liner 736 that was latterly named the Queen Elizabeth II.

MICHAEL AND BILLY

Sectarianism is when religious differences are used as an excuse for prejudice. It can take the form of name-calling, joke-telling, songs, chants and other forms of verbal abuse and even violence. We should never underestimate the power of words and role models in the shaping of our futures and in how we can shape the futures of others.

Afterword for teachers

First and foremost this is a poetry collection with illustrations. One that encourages P5s – young adults, to read and enjoy poetry. But it can also be used as a teaching resource. The following shows what I had in mind when pulling these poems and illustrations together and why I am making the distinction between poetry and resource.

Over recent years I've worked in primary and secondary schools and also in the further education sector, teaching creative writing and literacy. I've worked with children and adults of varying abilities, giving students and pupils various tasks and stimuli to encourage them to not only write but to write creatively.

After looking at the various age groups and their engagement/non-engagement with language, it became obvious to me that when the primary pupils were given tasks, in general they had a connection with language and creativity that encouraged them to engage with these tasks. This engagement, for various reasons, seems to lessen dramatically when they move on to secondary, then adulthood.

It's obvious that we must engage our readers and writers when they are young and endeavour to stimulate them to maintain that engagement into their adult years.

A philosopher once asked the question: 'If we didn't have any sensory experience of the world, would we have a thought in our head?' He was arguing on the premise that all thought is a result of sensory experience, If this is the case, then if a writer captures sensory experience that in turn is exposed to the reader then the reader will be engaged. There are many sides to this debate but nevertheless there's no denying the link with sensory experience and engagement.

I've noticed that by far the most engaging creative writing element is sensual imagery and if pupils and students can recognise this then they can begin to engage readers into their created world, and also they then recognise themselves that when they read writing written in this manner, they can receive stimulation and most importantly connect with the enjoyment of reading.

The poems in this collection have been written in the main using sensory imagery, and chronologically ordered, content-wise and stylistically, to initially engage and encourage readers when they are at the upper primary stage, then to maintain that engagement into their becoming young adults.

The use of illustrations is intrinsic in the book's structure, as they not only complement the words but also engage the readers, being a medium other than words, with elements of puzzle that ensure the reader looks closer and therefore absorbs the imagery on a word level and on a picture level. A cross-fertilisation of stimuli is the result.

Workshops can be used to explore the subjects covered in the poems and illustrations where students can discuss, draw, write and take part in drama improvisation.

A book to engage the child, the adult within the child, the child within the adult and also the adult – that's the goal of this collection that hopefully can be shared by different generations of readers.

Brian Whittingham

Further information and teaching resources can be found at
www.brianwhittingham.co.uk